MY COLORS

Written and illustrated by

ORNA

Copyright © 2016 ORNA

BLUE

RED

YELLOW

BLACK

WHITE

MIX
BLUE
WITH
YELLOW

GREEN

MIX
RED
WITH
BLUE

PURPLE

MIX
RED
WITH
YELLOW

ORANGE

MIX
BLACK
WITH
WHITE

GREY

MIX
BLUE
WITH
WHITE

LIGHT BLUE

MIX
RED
WITH
WHITE

PINK

MIX

BLACK

WITH

ORANGE

BROWN

BLUE LIGHT BLUE
RED PINK
YELLOW
BLACK GREY
WHITE
ORANGE
GREEN BROWN
PURPLE

www.ingramcontent.com/pod-product-compliance
Lightning Source LLC
Chambersburg PA
CBHW041317180526
45172CB00004B/1130